A CHILD'S
CHRISTMAS
IN WALES

A Child's Christmas in Wales

Dylan Thomas

Illustrated by Marian Bantjes

One Christmas was so much like another, in those years around the sea-town corner now, out of all sound except the distant speaking of the voices I sometimes hear a moment before sleep, that I can never remember whether it snowed for six days and six nights when I was twelve or whether it snowed for twelve days and twelve nights when I was six.

All the Christmases roll down towards the two-tongued sea, like a cold and headlong moon bundling down the sky that was our street; and they stop at the rim of the ice-edged, fish-freezing waves, and I plunge my hands in the snow and bring out whatever I can find. In goes my hand into that wool-white bell-tongued ball of holidays resting at the rim of the carol-singing sea, and out come Mrs. Prothero and the firemen.

It was on the afternoon of the day of Christmas Eve, and I was in Mrs. Prothero's garden, waiting for cats, with her son Jim. It was snowing. It was always snowing at Christmas. December, in my memory, is white as Lapland, though there were no reindeers. But there were cats. Patient, cold and callous, our hands wrapped in socks, we waited to snowball the cats. Sleek and long as jaguars and horrible-whiskered, spitting and snarling, they would slink and sidle over the white back-garden walls,

and the lynx-eyed hunters, Jim and I,
fur-capped and moccasined trappers
from Hudson Bay, off Mumbles Road,
would hurl our deadly snowballs at the
green of their eyes.

The wise cats never appeared.
We were so still, Eskimo-footed arctic marksmen in the muffling silence of the eternal snows—eternal, ever since Wednesday—that we never heard Mrs. Prothero's first cry from her igloo at the bottom of the garden. Or, if we heard it at all, it was, to us, like the far-off challenge of our enemy and prey, the neighbor's polar cat. But soon the voice grew louder. "Fire!" cried Mrs. Prothero, and she beat the dinner-gong.

And we ran down the garden, with the snowballs in our arms, towards the house; and smoke, indeed, was pouring out of the dining-room, and the gong was bombilating, and Mrs. Prothero was announcing ruin like a town crier in Pompeii. This was better than all the cats in Wales standing on the wall in a row. We bounded into the house, laden with snowballs, and stopped at the open door of the smoke-filled room.

Something was burning all right;
perhaps it was Mr. Prothero, who
always slept there after midday dinner
with a newspaper over his face.
But he was standing in the middle of
the room, saying, "A fine Christmas!"
and smacking at the smoke with a
slipper. "Call the fire brigade," cried
Mrs. Prothero as she beat the gong.

   "They won't be there," said Mr.
Prothero, "it's Christmas."

There was no fire to be seen, only clouds of smoke and Mr. Prothero standing in the middle of them, waving his slipper as though he were conducting.

"Do something," he said.

And we threw all our snowballs into the smoke—I think we missed Mr. Prothero—and ran out of the house to the telephone box.

"Let's call the police as well," Jim said.

"And the ambulance."

"And Ernie Jenkins, he likes fires."

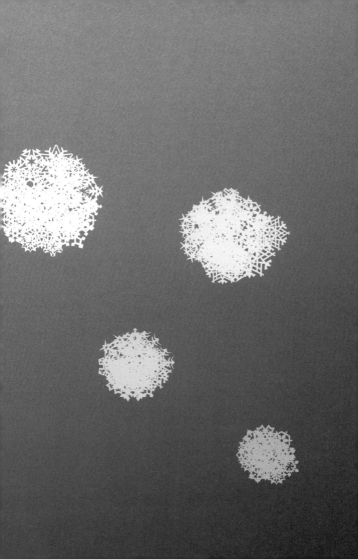

But we only called the fire brigade, and soon the fire engine came and three tall men in helmets brought a hose into the house and Mr. Prothero got out just in time before they turned it on. Nobody could have had a noisier Christmas Eve. And when the firemen turned off the hose and were standing in the wet, smoky room, Jim's aunt, Miss Prothero, came downstairs and peered in at them. Jim and I waited, very quietly, to hear what she would say to them. She said the right thing, always. She looked at the three tall firemen in their shining helmets, standing among the smoke and cinders and dissolving snowballs, and she said: "Would you like anything to read?"

Years and years ago, when I was a boy,
when there were wolves in Wales,
and birds the color of red-flannel
petticoats whisked past the harp-
shaped hills, when we sang and
wallowed all night and day in caves
that smelt like Sunday afternoons in
damp front farmhouse parlors, and we
chased, with the jawbones of deacons,
the English and the bears, before the
motor car, before the wheel,

before the duchess-faced horse, when
we rode the daft and happy hills
bareback, it snowed and it snowed.
But here a small boy says:

*"It snowed last year, too. I made a snowman
and my brother knocked it down and I knocked
my brother down and then we had tea."*

"But that was not the same snow,"
I say. "Our snow was not only shaken
from whitewash buckets down the sky,
it came shawling out of the ground
and swam and drifted out of the arms
and hands and bodies of the trees;
snow grew overnight on the roofs of
the houses like a pure and grandfather
moss, minutely white-ivied the
walls and settled on the postman,
opening the gate, like a dumb, numb
thunderstorm of white, torn Christmas
cards."

"Were there postmen then, too?"

"With sprinkling eyes and wind-cherried noses, on spread, frozen feet they crunched up to the doors and mittened on them manfully. But all that the children could hear was a ringing of bells."

"You mean that the postman went rat-a-tat-tat and the doors rang?"

"I mean that the bells that the children could hear were inside them."

"I only hear thunder sometimes, never bells."

"There were church bells, too."

"Inside them?"

"No, no, no, in the bat-black, snow-white belfries, tugged by bishops and storks. And they rang their tidings over the bandaged town, over the frozen foam of the powder and ice-cream hills, over the crackling sea.
It seemed that all the churches boomed for joy under my window; and the weathercocks crew for Christmas, on our fence."

"Get back to the postmen."

"They were just ordinary postmen,
fond of walking and dogs and
Christmas and the snow. They knocked
on the doors with blue knuckles...."

"Ours has got a black knocker...."

"And then they stood on the white
Welcome mat in the little, drifted
porches and huffed and puffed,
making ghosts with their breath,
and jogged from foot to foot like
small boys wanting to go out."

"And then the presents?"

"And then the Presents, after the Christmas box. And the cold postman, with a rose on his button-nose, tingled down the tea-tray-slithered run of the chilly glinting hill. He went in his

ice-bound boots like a man on
fishmonger's slabs. He wagged his bag
like a frozen camel's hump, dizzily
turned the corner on one foot, and,
by God, he was gone."

"Get back to the Presents."

"There were the Useful Presents:
engulfing mufflers of the old coach
days, and mittens made for giant
sloths; zebra scarfs of a substance like
silky gum that could be tug-o'-warred
down to the galoshes; blinding tam-o'-
shanters like patchwork tea cozies and
bunny-suited busbies and balaclavas
for victims of head-shrinking tribes;
from aunts who always wore wool
next to the skin there were mustached
and rasping vests that made you
wonder why the aunts had any skin
left at all; and once I had a little

crocheted nose bag from an aunt now, alas, no longer whinnying with us. And pictureless books in which small boys, though warned with quotations not to, *would* skate on Farmer Giles' pond and did and drowned; and books that told me everything about the wasp, except why."

"Go on to the Useless Presents."

"Bags of moist and many-colored jelly
babies and a folded flag and a false
nose and a tram-conductor's cap and a
machine that punched tickets and
rang a bell; never a catapult; once, by
a mistake that no one could explain,
a little hatchet; and a celluloid duck
that made, when you pressed it,
a most unducklike sound, a mewing
moo that an ambitious cat might
make who wished to be a cow;
and a painting book in which I could
make the grass, the trees, the sea
and the animals any color I pleased,
and still the dazzling sky-blue sheep
are grazing in the red field under

the rainbow-billed and pea-green birds. Hardboileds, toffee, fudge and allsorts, crunches, cracknel, humbugs, glaciers, marzipan, and butterwelsh for the Welsh. And troops of bright tin soldiers who, if they could not fight, could always run. And Snakes-and-Families and Happy Ladders. And Easy Hobbi-Games for Little Engineers, complete with instructions. Oh, easy for Leonardo! And a whistle to make the dogs bark to wake up the old man next door to make him beat on the wall with his stick to shake our picture off the wall. And a packet of cigarettes: you put one in your mouth and you stood at the corner of the street and you waited for hours, in vain, for an old lady to scold you for smoking a cigarette, and then with a smirk you ate it. And then it was breakfast under the balloons."

"Were there Uncles, like in our house?"

"There are always Uncles at Christmas. The same Uncles. And on Christmas mornings, with dog-disturbing whistle and sugar fags, I would scour the swathed town for the news of the little world, and find always a dead bird by the Post Office or the white deserted swings; perhaps a robin, all but one of his fires out. Men and women wading or scooping back from chapel, with taproom noses and wind-bussed cheeks, all albinos, huddled their stiff black jarring feathers against the irreligious snow. Mistletoe hung from the gas brackets in all the front parlors; there was sherry and walnuts and bottled beer and crackers by the dessertspoons; and cats in their fur-abouts watched the fires; and the high-heaped fire spat, all ready for the chestnuts and the mulling pokers.

Some few large men sat in the front parlors, without their collars, Uncles almost certainly, trying their new cigars, holding them out judiciously at arms' length, returning them to their mouths, coughing, then holding them out again as though waiting for the explosion; and some few small aunts, not wanted in the kitchen, nor anywhere else for that matter, sat on the very edges of their chairs, poised and brittle, afraid to break, like faded cups and saucers."

Not many those mornings trod the
piling streets: an old man always,
fawn-bowlered, yellow-gloved and,
at this time of year, with spats of snow,
would take his constitutional to the
white bowling green and back, as he
would take it wet or fire on Christmas
Day or Doomsday; sometimes two
hale young men, with big pipes
blazing, no overcoats and wind-blown
scarfs, would trudge, unspeaking,
down to the forlorn sea, to work up
an appetite, to blow away the fumes,
who knows, to walk into the waves

until nothing of them was left but the two curling smoke clouds of their inextinguishable briars. Then I would be slap-dashing home, the gravy smell of the dinners of others, the bird smell, the brandy, the pudding and mince, coiling up to my nostrils, when out of a snow-clogged side lane would come a boy the spit of myself, with a pink-tipped cigarette and the violet past of a black eye, cocky as a bullfinch, leering all to himself.

I hated him on sight and sound,
and would be about to put my dog
whistle to my lips and blow him off
the face of Christmas when suddenly
he, with a violet wink, put *his* whistle
to *his* lips and blew so stridently,
so high, so exquisitely loud, that
gobbling faces, their cheek bulged
with goose, would press against their
tinsled windows, the whole length of
the white echoing street.

For dinner we had turkey and blazing pudding, and after dinner the Uncles sat in front of the fire, loosened all buttons, put their large moist hands over their watch chains, groaned a little and slept. Mothers, aunts and sisters scuttled to and fro, bearing tureens. Auntie Bessie, who had already been frightened, twice, by a clock-work mouse, whimpered at the sideboard and had some elderberry wine. The dog was sick. Auntie Dosie had to have three aspirins, but Auntie Hannah, who liked port, stood in the middle of the snowbound back yard, singing like a big-bosomed thrush. I would blow up balloons to see how big they would blow up to; and when they burst, which they all did, the Uncles jumped and rumbled. In the rich and heavy afternoon, the Uncles breathing like dolphins and the snow descending, I would sit among festoons and Chinese lanterns and nibble dates and try to make a model man-o'-war, following the Instructions for Little Engineers, and produce what might be mistaken for a sea-going tramcar.

Or I would go out, my bright new boots squeaking, into the white world, on to the seaward hill, to call on Jim and Dan and Jack and to pad through the still streets, leaving huge deep footprints on the hidden pavements.

"I bet people will think there've been hippos."

"What would you do if you saw a hippo coming down our street?"

"I'd go like this, bang! I'd throw him over the railings and roll him down the hill and then I'd tickle him under the ear and he'd wag his tail."

"What would you do if you saw *two* hippos?"

Iron-flanked and bellowing he-hippos clanked and battered through the scudding snow towards us as we passed Mr. Daniel's house.

"Let's post Mr. Daniel a snowball through his letter box."

"Let's write things in the snow."

"Let's write, 'Mr. Daniel looks like a spaniel' all over his lawn."

Or we walked on the white shore.

"Can the fishes see it's snowing?"

The silent one-clouded heavens drifted on to the sea. Now we were snow-blind travelers lost on the north hills, and vast dewlapped dogs, with flasks round their necks, ambled and shambled up to us, baying "Excelsior." We returned home through the poor streets where only a few children fumbled with bare red fingers in the wheel-rutted snow and cat-called after us, their voices fading away, as we trudged uphill, into the cries of the dock birds and the hooting of ships out in the whirling bay.

And then, at tea the recovered Uncles would be jolly; and the ice cake loomed in the center of the table like a marble grave. Auntie Hannah laced her tea with rum, because it was only once a year.

Bring out the tall tales now that we told by the fire as the gaslight bubbled like a diver. Ghosts whooed like owls in the long nights when I dared not look over my shoulder; animals lurked in the cubbyhole under the stairs where the gas meter ticked. And I remember that we went singing carols once, when there wasn't the shaving of a moon to light the flying streets. At the end of a long road was

a drive that led to a large house,
and we stumbled up the darkness of
the drive that night, each one of us
afraid, each one holding a stone in his
hand in case, and all of us too brave
to say a word. The wind through
the trees made noises as of old and
unpleasant and maybe webfooted
men wheezing in caves. We reached
the black bulk of the house.

"What shall we give them? Hark the Herald?"

"No," Jack said, "Good King Wenceslas. I'll count three."

One, two, three, and we began to sing,
our voices high and seemingly distant
in the snow-felted darkness round the
house that was occupied by nobody
we knew. We stood close together,
near the dark door.

    Good King Wenceslas looked out
    On the Feast of Stephen ...

And then a small, dry voice, like the
voice of someone who has not spoken
for a long time, joined our singing:
a small, dry, eggshell voice from the
other side of the door: a small, dry
voice through the keyhole. And when
we stopped running we were outside
our house; the front room was lovely;
balloons floated under the hot-water-
bottle-gulping gas; everything was
good again and shone over the town.

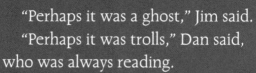

"Perhaps it was a ghost," Jim said.

"Perhaps it was trolls," Dan said, who was always reading.

"Let's go in and see if there's any jelly left," Jack said. And we did that.

Always on Christmas night there was music. An uncle played the fiddle, a cousin sang "Cherry Ripe," and another uncle sang "Drake's Drum." It was very warm in the little house. Auntie Hannah, who had got on to the parsnip wine, sang a song about Bleeding Hearts and Death, and then another in which she said her heart was like a Bird's Nest; and then everybody laughed again; and then I went to bed.

Looking through my bedroom
window, out into the moonlight and
the unending smoke-colored snow,
I could see the lights in the windows
of all the other houses on our hill and
hear the music rising from them up
the long, steadily falling night.
I turned the gas down, I got into bed.
I said some words to the close and
holy darkness, and then I slept.

Design and illustrations by Marian Bantjes

First published in this edition in 2016 (ISBN 978-0-8112-2622-6)
Manufactured in the United States of America
New Directions Books are printed on acid-free paper

Library of Congress Cataloging-in-Publication Data
Thomas, Dylan, 1914–1953.
A child's Christmas in Wales / by Dylan Thomas.
ISBN: 978-0-8112-1731-6 (pbk; alk. paper)
1. Thomas, Dylan, 1914–1953—Childhood and youth.
2. Thomas, Dylan, 1914–1953—Homes and haunts—Wales.
3. Poets, Welsh—20th century—Biography. 4. Christmas—Wales.
5. Wales—Social life and customs. I. Title.
PR6039.H52C48 2007
821'.912—dc22
[B]   2007024727

10 9 8 7 6 5 4 3 2 1

New Directions Books are published for James Laughlin
by New Directions Publishing Corporation
80 Eighth Avenue, New York 10011